*God's
Love Letters
to You*

ALSO BY DR. LARRY CRABB

SPIRITUAL GROWTH BOOKS

66 Love Letters

Becoming a True Spiritual
Community

Connecting

Finding God

God of My Father

Inside Out

Marriage Builder

Men & Women

Real Church

Shattered Dreams

Silence of Adam

SoulTalk

The PAPA Prayer

The Pressure's Off

Understanding People

Understanding Who You Are

COUNSELING SERIES

Basic Principles of Biblical
Counseling

Effective Biblical Counseling

Encouragement

AUDIO CDs

A Liberating Look at Gender

Chess Players or Poets

Christian Counseling and the
New Way

Experiencing the Trinity

Freedom Series

The Church I Want to Be Part Of

The Unique Value of Small Groups

To the Children

What Every Christian Counselor
Needs to Know

A Christian Response to
Homosexuality

How Not to Become an Atheist

SoulTalk

To the Husbands

Unpacking but Never Solving the
Mystery of Prayer

DVD CURRICULUM

The SoulCare Experience

God's Love Letters to You

A 40-Day Devotional Experience

DR. LARRY CRABB

THOMAS NELSON
Since 1798

NASHVILLE   DALLAS   MEXICO CITY   RIO DE JANEIRO

Published in Nashville, Tennessee, by Thomas Nelson. Thomas Nelson is a registered trademark of Thomas Nelson, Inc.

Thomas Nelson, Inc. titles may be purchased in bulk for educational, business, fund-raising, or sales promotional use. For information, please e-mail SpecialMarkets@ThomasNelson.com.

Unless otherwise noted, Scripture quotations are taken from the Holy Bible, New International Version®, NIV®. © 1973, 1978, 1984 by Biblica, Inc.™ Used by permission of Zondervan. All rights reserved worldwide. www.zondervan.com.

Scripture quotations marked MSG are from *The Message* by Eugene H. Peterson. © 1993, 1994, 1995, 1996, 2000, 2001, 2002. Used by permission of NavPress Publishing Group. All rights reserved.

Scripture quotations marked NKJV are from the New King James Version®. © 1982 by Thomas Nelson, Inc. Used by permission. All rights reserved.

Library of Congress Cataloging-in-Publication Data

Crabb, Lawrence J.
  God's love letters to you : a 40-day devotional experience / Larry Crabb.
    p. cm.
  ISBN 978-0-8499-4647-9 (pbk.)
  1. Bible--Devotional literature. I. Title.
  BS491.5.C695 2011
  242'.5--dc22

                              2010053982

Printed in the United States of America

11 12 13 14 RRD 9 8 7 6 5 4 3 2 1

To my grandchildren,
Josie, Jake, Kaitlyn, Keira, Kenzie.
May the God who is my life make each of your lives beautiful.
Never forget: your Pop-Pop loves you.

Contents

Contents

Acknowledgments

*D*ebbie, you championed this project with a vision for how God could use it. Your excitement is contagious. To you and the great Nelson team, a big thank-you.

Andi, Kep, and Darla, none of what God is doing through NewWay Ministries would be happening without your creative, tireless, and dedicated efforts. You believe in our ministry. That keeps me going more than you can realize.

Kent and Karla, on short notice you came up with reflective questions for each day's reading that capture the Spirit's movement and will open many hearts to move with Him. And your suggestions for a daily prayer of response so obviously came from your passionate longing to surrender to the Spirit's deepest work in your hearts. I know something of the price you pay. Walking with you both on the narrow road is one of my greatest privileges and deepest joys.

And Rachael, no writer more painfully realizes and profoundly appreciates the sacrifices you make to so warmly and patiently support what we both believe God has called me to do. Your loving heart is a treasure to your family, an unmatched blessing to me, and an unceasing delight to God. I love you.

Hearing God's Life Words

*W*ords have power. A single sentence can mark a person for life. A careless word, a slip of the tongue, a thoughtless remark can spark a blaze that wounds the heart and scorches the soul, even if the word, slip, or remark seems insignificant and relatively harmless.

When I was thirteen years old, a friend was shooting baskets with me on a basketball court. After another of my jump shots missed, he casually commented, "You look more like you're lifting a barbell than shooting a basketball."

I quickly switched to tennis. A chance remark, a casual comment, a passing observation—and I pretty much gave up basketball.

A thoughtful word carries equally powerful potential. An encouraging sentence, a sensitive remark from someone who sees you and cares, can flood your heart with joy and energize your soul to move ahead toward your God-appointed destiny.

When I wrote *66 Love Letters*, I listened to God's Spirit speak to me in each book of the Bible. I believed then (and believe more strongly now) that all sixty-six love letters were filled with *life words*.

Probably like you, I've heard my share of *death* words:

some like the statement my friend made on the basketball court, and some, far more hurtful, from friends who turned against me (perhaps after I had hurt them). Some death words come from the father of lies and too often echo somewhere deep in my soul. Some come from folks who love me who intended to speak life words that I managed to hear as death words.

The well-meaning parent, the loving spouse, the sincerely appreciative son or daughter, and the devoted friend—let alone the mean-spirited parent, the rejecting spouse, the sullen son or daughter, the betraying friend—will occasionally speak words intended to bring pain.

Only one Father, only one Bridegroom and Friend, only one Counselor and Companion can be counted on to *always* speak life words. But God's way of thinking and His way of loving are so far above us—and so different sometimes from what we think they should be—that His way of speaking life can feel harsh, even insensitive and uncaring. And for good reason: His words of life speak death to what is in us that needs to die.

Sometimes we foolishly try to keep alive what He wants to kill; we've somehow gotten the idea that the thing trying to kill us will actually bring us life. So when God speaks words of death to what is killing us, we don't easily hear loving words that are stirring up real life within us.

If I have one prayer for this little book of devotional readings, it is this: I pray that people across the world, people of every age, of every color and creed, people in any circumstance, followers of Jesus or not-yet followers of Jesus, married, divorced, or single, in the hospital or on vacation, will hear the love story God is telling us in words that reveal His heart, words that speak life into ours.

After more than forty years of counseling and walking with thousands on their spiritual journeys, I am convinced that love reaches into the heart more deeply than evil, that words of life have the power to bring healing to souls damaged and seemingly defeated by death words. And I believe there is only one reliable source of love and life words, the living God of love, and that every word in the Bible is spoken by the God who speaks only life into those who listen and believe.

This book offers forty selected passages from *66 Love Letters* for daily reading. A few thought-provoking questions follow each passage to help you pause to reflect on the life words from God. I then suggest words of request and response to bring before God in prayer.

May these devotional readings create an opportunity to lay aside and disempower any death words you've heard as your heart is awakened and your soul is enlivened with words of life, from Life Himself.

My prayer for you and for me as we listen to God is this:

Father, Son, and Holy Spirit, mark us for life with Your words of life. Undo the power of every death word we've heard. Empower us to speak life into others by speaking life into us. Pour living water into our parched souls. Thrill us with the privilege of relating to others in a way that reveals Your heart to them and releases Your life into them through the words we speak. Thank You for speaking life into us. Open our hearts to hear Your words and to receive them. In Jesus' name, amen.

Day One: Genesis

I HAVE A PLAN: TRUST ME

Then Joseph said to his brothers, ". . . God will surely come to your aid and take you up out of this land to the land he promised on oath to Abraham, Isaac and Jacob . . . God will surely come to your aid."

—GENESIS 50:24–25

*G*od says: I want you to realize that I never underestimated how thoroughly you'd mess up your life or how painfully you would struggle and suffer, and I don't want you to underestimate your failures or struggles either. They're all part of the story I'm telling.

But neither have I underestimated My determination or ability to enter both the mess you've made and the pain you feel, then turn everything around. I can, and I will, make everything good again. Never, ever underestimate Me. I have a plan, a very good one, and it will move ahead to completion. Guaranteed! Trust Me. Why? Because I love you even when you're messing up badly. I love you in the middle of your pain even though I don't relieve it as quickly as you wish. I am worthy of your trust, no matter what happens in your life. I have a good plan, and nothing will stop Me from carrying it to completion.

You must live now in the tension between anguish and hope.

TAKE A MOMENT TO REFLECT

❁ Recall a mess you've made at some time in some area of your life and how God may have entered into that mess with you. How has the experience added to your life story?

❁ What possible reason could God have for not relieving our troubles more quickly? How do the difficulties we face serve the purposes of God's love?

❁ What do you believe is the center of God's good plan for your life now, before you get to heaven?

TAKE A MOMENT TO PRAY

God, it's hard to believe that everything that goes wrong in my life is part of Your good plan. It's even harder to believe that everything I do wrong can somehow lead to something good. God, I believe . . . a little. Help me believe more. In Jesus' name, amen.

Day Two:
Exodus

CONSIDER THE LENGTHS I GO TO,
JUST TO BE WITH YOU

———— ••◦◦❦◦◦•• ————

Let them make Me a sanctuary, that I may dwell among them.
—EXODUS 25:8 NKJV

*G*od says: I can and I will detach you from everything that numbs your sacred hunger for Me and makes you feel hungrier for something other than Me.

You will never on this earth depend fully enough on My power to live exactly as I want you to live. When you see how particular I am about all the rules you should obey but never do, let the weight of My holiness draw you into the delights of My love. I still want to be with you.

Don't ever forget: I do have a plan, a plan to make you deliriously happy in the circle of My love. As you read Exodus 25–40, where I record all those architectural details about the tabernacle, realize the lengths I'm willing to go to be with you. Imagine Me, the God of the universe, clothed in splendor and arrayed in glory, living in, by My standards, a simple tent set up in a barren wilderness. Sure, it was fancy, but compare it to what you imagine heaven to be. But that's where I lived, just to be near people like you.

As you consider all the laws I gave that you've never kept, and as you see My willingness to go camping to be with My people, know this: I will do whatever it takes to fully restore My family and to be with them forever.

TAKE A MOMENT TO REFLECT

❀ Unknowingly, we often find ways to numb our hunger for God with things like coffee, shopping, sex, sports—you name it. In what ways might you numb your sacred hunger?

❀ How is our failure to keep God's rules intended to draw us into the delights of His love?

❀ What does the final sentence—"I will do whatever it takes to fully restore My family and to be with them forever"—provoke in your heart?

TAKE A MOMENT TO PRAY

Father, give us the courage to identify and live in our deepest hunger for You. Redeem the truth that You as a holy God desire to live with us even amid our sin. In Jesus' name, amen.

Day Three: Leviticus

Solving your worst problem

———— ✤ ————

Both the one who makes men holy and those who
are made holy are of the same family.
—Hebrews 2:11

*G*od says: You want Me to solve your problems, but you don't know what your worst problem is, the one responsible for all the others. You don't yet realize that distance from Me is the most lethal problem you have.

You assume we're doing just fine together while you run off, trying to make life work for you, and you expect Me to cooperate. When you read Leviticus, notice that I never solve anyone's secondary problems. In all those verses about skin infection, for example, I never prescribed ointment or simply cured the disease, which I easily could have done. I simply told people they couldn't enter My Presence with an oozing sore. The issue was worship and intimacy with Me, not health, wealth, or personal comfort.

So many people miss that. They identify their needs and then view Me as a God who wants them satisfied and happy before I deal with their unholiness. But because I love them—and you—I've made a way for you to revolve your life around Me as your first thing. Everything else—your marriage, your checkbook, your self-esteem, your cancer—is a second thing. When the first thing (namely, Me) is in first place in your life, every second thing will be taken care of.

You've got a long way to go before that's true in your life, but I have a plan to get you there, to make you holy.

TAKE A MOMENT TO REFLECT

❀ If you didn't feel the need to "spiritualize" or worry about what others think, how would you define what your worst problem is?

❀ What are some of the second things in your life that you long for God to address?

❀ The second things of our lives often take priority over what God says matters most. How would you describe, after reading these words, what God's deepest commitment is in our lives?

TAKE A MOMENT TO PRAY

God, I would settle for far less than Your commitment to make me holy as You are. Too often my commitment is to use You to make my life comfortable. Forgive me. In Jesus' name, amen.

Day Four:
Numbers

PERSEVERING ON THE ROUGH
ROAD TO MY PARTY

These are all warning markers—danger!—in our history books,
written down so that we don't repeat their mistakes . . . Forget
about self-confidence; it's useless. Cultivate God-confidence.

—1 CORINTHIANS 10:11–12 MSG

*G*od says: The road to life is rough. You will begin every new adventure in life with naive hope and excitement. Every wedding will begin with passion, then move into problems. Every decorated nursery will receive a baby who will present unanticipated challenges. Every church plant, every new ministry, every small group starts with happy hopes. Everything you do, no matter how well organized and well intentioned, will run into trouble.

The road to life will expose you to terrible failure and crushing conflict. But only that road leads to the life you want, the life I give you. Spiritual leaders who teach that I am here to solve your problems and make your lives comfortable and prosperous underestimate the energy (and badly misunderstand the nature) of unholiness in the human heart that I must severely deal with to get you to My party.

And that underestimation leads them to underestimate the severity of My love. My servant C. S. Lewis got it right: I'm not safe, but I am good. I will not coddle you any more than a good surgeon only hugs a cancer-stricken child. I will not coddle you, but I will purify you. And that takes more, not less, than a hug.

TAKE A MOMENT TO REFLECT

❀ How do you respond to the statement that everything you do "will run into trouble"?

❀ Where have you known this to be true?

❀ What makes it difficult to believe that the road to life inevitably goes through "terrible failure and crushing conflict"?

❀ What are you assuming is the deepest problem of the human heart when you would rather be coddled than purified?

TAKE A MOMENT TO PRAY

Lord God, thank You for Your dogged commitment to purify me and get me to Your party. Open my eyes to see where I am more committed to my comfort than my holiness. I ask in Jesus' name, amen.

Day Five: Deuteronomy

I'm faithful to you anyway

---

*He brought us out from there to bring us in and give us the
land that he promised on oath to our forefathers.*

—Deuteronomy 6:23

*G*od says: I am the only true God. There is none other. When you don't like what I'm doing, there is no plan B. I brought you out to bring you in. You were locked in the prison of self-centeredness, just as Israel was in painful bondage to Egypt, where all they could think about was themselves—how can we get a better life? Not, how can we love God?

I brought you out of that prison to bring you into the freedom of love. If you love Me only when I immediately satisfy your desires, your love is merely one more form of self-centeredness. Your love becomes trust only when you choose to believe that I brought you out of something bad to bring you into something good before you experience that something good. Then your love is sustained by confidence in My character, not by enjoyment of current blessings.

I ask nothing of you but that kind of love, which includes respecting Me for who I am, following Me wherever I lead, serving Me with your whole heart, and obeying every command I give.

But that's asking something neither you nor Israel could give. You are not capable of loving Me like that. No one can please me unless I put the life of My Son, who always pleases Me, into his or her heart. And that's what I promised to do. That's what I have done. I'm faithful to faithless people. Believe that, and know that now you can be faithful to Me, not perfectly, but you can learn to live in rhythm with My Son, a little more gracefully each day.

TAKE A MOMENT TO REFLECT

❀ Given the verse in today's reading, out of what do you think God is bringing us? Into what do you think God longs to bring us?

❀ Think of a situation that currently "ties you up in knots." How does the sentence, "Then your love is sustained by confidence in My character, not by enjoyment of current blessings," speak to that situation?

❀ What do you believe is the ruling passion at the heart of every redeemed image bearer?

TAKE A MOMENT TO PRAY

Oh, Father, I would easily settle for a blessed life here . . . trying to use You to cooperate with my agendas. You have such a higher vision for me than I am capable of pulling off in my own strength. Thank You for having done all the work, which includes giving me a heart that loves You as Your Son does. In Jesus' name, amen.

Day Six:
Joshua

VICTORY REQUIRES DISCERNMENT

---

*Be strong and of good courage; do not be afraid, nor be
dismayed, for the LORD your God is with you wherever you go.*
—JOSHUA 1:9 NKJV

$\mathcal{G}$od says: Invite Christians to live for Jesus and imply that the Christian life is all about blessings, about entering a land filled with milk and honey with no real battles, and they all will come forward. Churches that never deal with the real fight that following My Son requires often grow large but mostly with small Christians.

Defeating their enemies involved conflict for Israel, failure, and the need for discernment, just as it does in your life. Israel had to fight real battles with real swords that shed real blood. Some of the people, like Achan, preferred blessings to battle. That preference led to failure as it will in your life.

Discernment, too, is hard to come by. Even Joshua mistook an enemy for a friend, a terrible lack of discernment. And despite Joshua's best efforts, My people sometimes squabbled over their enjoyment of blessings. Pay attention to that. A spirit of entitlement and jealousy will plague you until you die. You'll need discernment to identify it, recognize it as wrong, and know how to navigate your way through it.

Your leaders, all of them, are imperfect, but you will need them to more effectively fight the real battle, to resist compromise and deception, and to enjoy your blessings without the spirit of entitlement corrupting your gratitude. Substantial victory is available in this life but only with struggles that remain until heaven.

TAKE A MOMENT TO REFLECT

❁ How would you define the real battle that following God's Son requires?

❁ Within our lives and our churches, we see conflict and failure as our enemies. How might these instead be the context for discerning the real enemy from which God seeks to free us?

❁ A spirit of entitlement exists in all of us (*God, You owe me an understanding spouse . . . children who follow You . . . good health . . . a fulfilling career*). It often only surfaces during times of prolonged pain and suffering. Where have you seen this spirit in your life?

TAKE A MOMENT TO PRAY

God, often my battles are about securing blessings that I believe I deserve. I long for Your discernment to be about the real fight within me and others that will lead us to gratitude. In Jesus' name, amen.

Day Seven:
Judges

UNDERSTANDING AUTHENTIC LOVE

———————•◦✦◦•———————

God is doing what is best for us, training us to live God's holy best.
—HEBREWS 12:10 MSG

*G*od says: I never heal superficially. Many of My people wish I did and think I do. I don't. My plan is to change you from the inside out, to change your motives—why you do what you do—and to change your impact on people so that how you relate to others will make them thirsty for Me and will draw them to dependence on Me.

When you love Me above all else, what you do will bring Me pleasure because your motives, though never pure, will be holy. And when you love others with an authenticity and passion that draw them toward Me, you will feel a little of the pleasure I feel.

Only when people look deeply into themselves will they truly repent. My people in Judges never repented. They remained in love with their own sense of well-being, with no understanding that love, real love, the love that defines Me, involves suffering the loss of well-being for the sake of another.

That lack of understanding is epidemic, not only in culture but in churches today. And it is in you. You and everyone else are inclined to depend on Me for the good life of blessings and to mistake that dependence for love. You're more afraid of losing the good life than of losing (or never gaining) a close relationship with Me. You do not yet see that being with Me is your greatest blessing, no matter what else may be happening in your life.

TAKE A MOMENT TO REFLECT

❀ It is far easier to expend our energy on our behavior, cleaning up the outside of the cup as indicated by Jesus in Matthew 23:25–26. What makes it difficult to turn and honestly face the motivation of our hearts?

❀ Based on the reading, what do you think true repentance involves?

❀ Unknowingly, what we call love is often intended to get something from another. Recognizing this can lead to another type of love. How would you define that love?

❀ As you reflect back over today's reading, what sentences create an anticipation that you could share in the pleasures of God?

TAKE A MOMENT TO PRAY

Lord, I long to see You as my greatest blessing. My priority is most often my own sense of well-being and not the well-being of others. Make me holy so that I may know a bit of the pleasure You know. In Jesus' name, amen.

Day Eight:
Ruth

MY LOVE CAN OVERCOME
ALL OBSTACLES

A full reward be given you by the LORD God of Israel,
under whose wings you have come for refuge.
—RUTH 2:12 NKJV

*G*od says: No matter what happens in your life, I can reach into your heart with the power to form you into someone who values Me above everyone and everything else. I am determined to reverse your values.

My plan has a happy ending, a wonderful finale far better than you can imagine, but the happy ending is only for the holy. I am committed to your holiness at any cost to Me, required by My nature, and at any cost to you, required by yours, and on whatever timetable is necessary. There are intractable obstacles I must overcome to make you holy. I deal with three in Ruth: natural disadvantages that to you seem more important to overcome than an unholy value system; shattered dreams that bring so much pain into your life that it's difficult to welcome the opportunity they provide for new levels of trust; and material resources that make it easy to disguise narcissism behind nonsacrificial generosity.

Ruth's life is a they-all-lived-happily-ever-after story, but it is not a parable of My power to make life comfortable; it is a parable of My power to make people holy. Know this: holiness and only holiness brings joy. No problem in your life, whether difficult problems such as disadvantages and loss, or agreeable problems, such as wealth, can stop My plan. Faith and hope together release love. And love is holiness. Hear what I'm saying in this love letter: no matter how dark the world around you, no matter how difficult the world inside you, My plan overcomes all obstacles to holiness.

TAKE A MOMENT TO REFLECT

❀ God's commitment to us is actually one of our deepest desires, which is to be holy (defined as the joy of relating like the Trinity). And yet we so easily and so often live to satisfy lesser desires. For what lesser desires do you settle that interfere with your deepest desire?

❀ Recall a natural disadvantage, a shattered dream, or a lost material resource. Given God's commitment to our holiness, how has He used this experience?

❀ We often define hope as wishing for a changed circumstance or the fulfillment of a desire. Based on today's reading, how would you define our true hope?

TAKE A MOMENT TO PRAY

Thank You, Lord, that Your vision and commitment to make me like Your Son are far bigger and more beautiful than my vision for myself. No matter how dark the world around me or how difficult the world inside me becomes, thank You that Your plan overcomes all obstacles to holiness. In Jesus' name, amen.

Day Nine:
1 Samuel

MOVING FROM EMPTINESS TO HOLINESS . . . TO LAUGHTER

---

*The people refused to obey the voice of Samuel;
and they said, "No, but we will have a king over
us, that we also may be like all the nations."*

—1 SAMUEL 8:19–20 NKJV

*G*od says: I'm aware that things go wrong in your life, that family and friends don't always treat you well, that nothing goes exactly as you want it to. I grieve with you over the pain that life causes you. But our priorities differ. You ask what will work to make your life better, to correct the injustice you suffer, to see to it that more things go as they should in your life. I want you to ask what holiness would look like in your situation, whatever it is, holiness that might not right the wrongs you suffer but that would let us enjoy each other.

I tell Samuel's story to let you see how Israel's spiritual leaders, when they saw trouble brewing at the end of Samuel's life, forgot Me—no, they rejected Me—and honored their own agenda to make life work according to their own wisdom. They insisted that Samuel appoint a human king, a king other than Me, to lead them. They wanted to fit in with the way other people ran their lives that seemed to be working for them. Israel had never had a king other than Me.

It hurts Me to see My people chase after a lesser good than knowing Me. It disturbs Me to watch them follow so-called proven methods to make good things happen and to value those managerial methods more than the holy and self-denying relating that pleases Me no matter what happens. You will understand My central message in this letter when you understand the tragedy of asking for a king other than Me. Following the ways of another may work for a season. It often leads to the shallow and short-lived laughter of pride in an accomplished agenda.

Following My ways will lead you through trouble and

emptiness to real laughter, to the laughter that only per-
sons in holy relationship can enjoy.

TAKE A MOMENT TO REFLECT

❀ Think of a difficult situation you are facing.
   What comes to mind when you ask, "Father,
   what would holiness look like in this situation?"
❀ What are the "managerial methods" you are
   tempted to follow in your relationships? What
   would it look like to relate with self-denying
   holiness no matter what happens?
❀ Holiness is often defined as sinlessness. While
   it certainly includes that, how would you
   further define the term based on the reading?

TAKE A MOMENT TO PRAY

Father, would You help me discover the joy of holy relating that defines You? Too often, my ways involve trying to
fix people and problems. Please give me a greater vision
that involves self-denying love. I humbly ask in Jesus'
name, amen.

Day Ten:
2 Chronicles

STRUGGLE TO TRUST ME

---

*Whatever prayer, whatever supplication is made by anyone . . .
then hear from heaven Your dwelling place, and forgive, and
give to everyone according to all his ways, whose heart You
know (for You alone know the hearts of the sons of men).*
—2 CHRONICLES 6:29–30 NKJV

*G*od says: Only when you see the moral evil in the human heart will you surrender to the mystery of My plan.

In this world, I am destroying moral evil in My people. In the next, I will eliminate natural evil. You must trust that I permit terrible things, natural evil that grieves My heart far more than yours, as part of the process of destroying the moral evil that offends My heart. In ways you cannot understand, I have the power and wisdom needed to move My plan forward through the evil of bombs and the injustice of suffering.

No matter how great your pain or how confusing and intense your suffering, live in the mystery of My love. Struggle to trust Me.

Do not live with the priority of making your life in this world as good as you can make it. You will suffer, at times unfairly, but you will be given what you need to enter strongly and wisely with supernatural love into every circumstance you face.

Doing so will be your joy, your hope, and your deepest fulfillment now as you look forward to a world where every child runs and laughs.

TAKE A MOMENT TO REFLECT

❀ In this world, God's commitment is to destroy
the moral evil in His people. What is required
for us to see this evil in our hearts?

❀ Why do you suppose it is a struggle to trust God?

❀ If our circumstances do not change, what is our
hope in the middle of the struggle?

TAKE A MOMENT TO PRAY

Lord God, *surrender* seems like an important word because I
so often have a different agenda than Yours. As You go
about the process of destroying the moral evil in me, I fear
that I won't see it as coming from Your heart of love. Help
me to trust You. In Jesus' name, amen.

Day Eleven:
Ezra

YOU *WILL* MAKE IT TO THE PARTY

Make confession to the LORD God of your fathers, and do His will.

—EZRA 10:11 NKJV

*G*od says: As soon as My people were settled in the land of promise, they rebuilt the altar on the same site where the original altar had rested. The altar of sacrifice symbolizes "yieldedness" to Me. To return to the narrow road, you need only surrender your will to Mine.

And as my beloved and for so long troubled servant John Bunyan described in *Pilgrim's Progress*, you will take the broad, more comfortable road through "bypath meadow." But know this: I will not leave you there!

Draw courage from this history.

I will strengthen you to fight the good fight and to finish well. You will make it to the party. There is always a way back from sin. Tears of hope will flow every time you experience My loving mercy when you fail.

I still love you. I will not give up on you. I have a plan.

TAKE A MOMENT TO REFLECT

❀ Our sin is never too big for God. We simply need to confess. What comes to mind that would be important for you to confess?

❀ Slowly reread the following thoughts as being from God's heart to yours:

- You will take the broad road, but I will not leave you there.
- I will strengthen you to fight the good fight and to finish well.
- You will make it to the party.
- There is always a way back from sin.
- I will not give up on you. I have a plan.

Of these five, which statement most resonates in your heart and why?

❀ What songs come to mind that you could sing to the Lord in response to His commitment to get you to the party?

TAKE A MOMENT TO PRAY

Father, thank You for the promise that we will make it to the party. Thank You for the assurance that there is always a way back from sin. Give us the strength to fight the good fight and to finish well. In Jesus' name, amen.

Day Twelve: Nehemiah

SMALL OBEDIENCE IS GREAT WORK

They were all trying to make us afraid, saying, "Their hands will be weakened in their work, and it will not be done." Now therefore, O God, strengthen my hands.

—NEHEMIAH 6:9 NKJV

*G*od says: Whatever anyone does out of a sincere desire to know Me and draw others to Me is a great work. And as you engage in that work, sometimes you will be energized as you catch a glimpse of My plan unfolding. More often, you won't. Either way, you are doing a great work.

Every father who repairs a leaky faucet and then prays with his kids before dinner is doing a great work. Every mother who prepares that dinner and joins in that prayer is doing a great work. Every single person who works hard to pay the rent and reads the Bible before bedtime is doing a great work.

I see it all. And I am pleased. Their reward is coming.

Whatever is done to know Me and make Me known, to advance My purposes, is a great work. And I will use every great work done by My people, no matter how small it seems, to further My great plan.

When you see the fullness of that plan and its end result, you will be plunged forever in a sea of joy.

TAKE A MOMENT TO REFLECT

- ✿ What enables our ordinary daily tasks to become great works?
- ✿ What lies would Satan like us to believe about what God is calling "great works"? How do God's thoughts and the world's ideas of a great work differ?
- ✿ How can your to-do list for today become part of God's great work?

TAKE A MOMENT TO PRAY

Father, may I not grow weary this day in well-doing, knowing that You say it matters. Like Nehemiah, I pray, "O God, strengthen my hands." In Jesus' name I pray, amen.

Day Thirteen: Psalms

THE STAKES ARE HIGH

———— ❧ ————

My soul clings to you; your right hand upholds me.

—PSALM 63:8

*G*od says: The Psalms are not an anesthetic. They are not a cup of hot chocolate on a cold night. They are the prayers of someone lost in a dark wood, shivering in bitter cold, unable to stand in fierce wind. They are the praise that flows from that person's heart when he abandons himself to Me for deliverance, when he trusts that My hand has grasped his and that I am leading him home, very slowly but very surely.

Face the hard questions that life requires you to ask. Gather with other travelers on the narrow road, pilgrims who acknowledge their confusion and feel their fears. Then, together, live those questions in My Presence.

Your tears will become the melody of a new song. Your darkness will become the window through which new light will appear. Your doubt will become new ground, solid ground, on which to stand. Your longing to feel your emptiness and ask your questions in My Presence, in the company of other authentic pilgrims, is good. That longing releases true worship and opens your ears to hear the music of heaven and to awkwardly but rhythmically begin to dance.

Decide, again and again, either to cling to Me as I am or reshape Me into who you want Me to be. The stakes are high. Either you will find yourself in finding Me, or you will lose yourself in creating Me to fit your foolish expectations.

Make the right choice.

TAKE A MOMENT TO REFLECT

❀ What makes it difficult to pray uncensored prayers, as the psalmists did?

❀ We often read scriptures like the Psalms to "anesthetize" us—from what?

❀ Where have you experienced the freedom of asking the difficult questions in the company of others in a way that has strengthened you? What is it about this process that makes it good?

❀ How are we in danger when we want to quickly bypass the hard questions of life to simply praise God?

TAKE A MOMENT TO PRAY

Lord, help me not to fear the hard questions that arise in the darkness of life. Instead, allow me to discover these times as a doorway into deeper relationship with You. Forgive me when I reshape You into the god I want You to be rather than allow You to be the God You are. In Jesus' name, amen.

Day Fourteen:
Song of Songs

COME TO MY FEAST OF LOVE

Love is invincible facing danger and death. Passion laughs at the terrors of hell. The fire of love stops at nothing—it sweeps everything before it.
—SONG OF SONGS 8:6 MSG

*G*od says: <u>I love you. I delight in you</u>. I will do what-ever it takes for you to enter into the exquisite, <u>life-defining pleasure of the communion My Son and I enjoy. I invite you into the feast of love</u>.

I am arousing the desire I put in every human heart to experience satisfaction in an undeserved relationship of love. To arouse desire without providing hope is cruel. To feel desire without hope of satisfaction is hell. Dante's words written over the door into Satan's world were apt: "Abandon hope, all ye who enter here."

But desire with hope is sweet. It is the abundant life . . . for now. I want you to nibble on the appetizers now. But to do so requires wisdom.

Relate authentically with Me.

Hurt and celebrate; lament and praise; weep and laugh.

Be all that you are without pretense in My Presence.

TAKE A MOMENT TO REFLECT

- ❀ How does facing the emptiness here aid in arousing our desire for the life-defining pleasure of the Trinity?
- ❀ How is the *abundant life* often defined? How is it defined differently in the reading today?
- ❀ Reread today's devotional and underline a phrase or two that entices you. What do you hear that is specifically for you?

TAKE A MOMENT TO PRAY

Father God, I so often struggle to believe that I am as loved as You say I am. Do what You need to so that truth may move from my head to my heart. Keep hope alive in me, and give me wisdom to know the truly abundant life. In Jesus' name, amen.

Day Fifteen: Jeremiah

I WILL RESCUE YOU

"Do not be afraid of them, for I am with you and
will rescue you," declares the LORD.

—JEREMIAH 1:8

*G*od says: I make no promise to protect you from suffering in this world. I do promise the power to believe in My goodness when bad things happen, the power to hope with confidence that a good plan is unfolding when nothing visible supports that hope, and the power to reveal the goodness of My love no matter how distraught or empty you feel.

Kierkegaard, my nineteenth-century Jeremiah, had it right. He confronted the culture of his day with these words: "Not until a person has become so wretched that his only wish, his only consolation, is to die—not until then does Christianity begin."

Without an ongoing consciousness of sin, any sense of nearness to Me is counterfeit. But with consciousness of sin, the fire of purifying holiness will sustain your faith. I rescued Jeremiah—and I will rescue you—from faithless unbelief, from hopeless despair, and from unloving self-obsession.

And now My Son has made it possible for you to live a life of abundant though severely tested faith, abundant though seriously challenged hope, and abundant though painfully sacrificial love.

TAKE A MOMENT TO REFLECT

❀ What is your internal response to God saying, "I make no promise to protect you from suffering in this world"?

❀ As you look again at the second and the last sentence in the reading, how are faith, hope, and love being defined? How is this consistent with what you have come to know on your journey?

❀ How does an "ongoing consciousness of sin" lead to a sustaining faith? How does it rescue a person from faithless, self-obsessed despair?

TAKE A MOMENT TO PRAY

Father, the fact that You do not promise to take it easy on us is what makes it hard to trust You. Please be gentle with me, yet do not stop until Your work is complete. When it is necessary, give me eyes to see how bad my sin is. Then give me hope and the resolve to love You by loving others. In Jesus' name, amen.

Day Sixteen:
Daniel

WHEN YOU'RE READY TO MEET ME

And there shall be a time of trouble, such as never
was since there was a nation, even to that time. And
at that time your people shall be delivered.

—DANIEL 12:1 NKJV

*G*od says: When I toss My children into the air, terror comes before delight. Put yourself in the place of My people in Daniel's day. They felt thrown into the air with no safety net beneath them. They couldn't see their God ready to catch them.

Jerusalem lay in ruins. They had no king. Heathens had entered the Holy of Holies and lived to bring home the sacred treasures they stole. And the theology of My people, all their expectations, crumbled.

The greatest danger My people face today is prosperity, blessings that reinforce the false hope that nothing serious will ever go wrong in their lives if they just keep believing, expecting, trusting, and smiling.

My people in Daniel's day were wrestling with hard questions that the prosperous church of today never asks.

When every expectation of how your life should turn out is shattered; when I seem to you like an indifferent, cold sovereign, a promise breaker, a useless God, an abandoning parent, rejoice! You are ready for the unveiling, to meet Me as I am.

TAKE A MOMENT TO REFLECT

- Put in your own words why prosperity and blessings can be dangerous. How is your view of God different in times of prosperity than in times of suffering?
- What would characterize our lives, our families, and our churches if we honored the life-shaping process that is going on in times of suffering and the shattering of our dreams?
- What questions surface in you when every expectation of how life should turn out is shattered?

TAKE A MOMENT TO PRAY

Father, help me not to scramble when my theology and my ideas about You crumble. Help me believe that You will reshape my understanding of You and of the faith. Give me the subtle wisdom to know that good times can be dangerous while difficult times provide an unexpected opportunity to meet the real You. In Jesus' name, amen.

Day Seventeen: Jonah

I DEMAND YOUR COOPERATION

I remembered God, and was troubled;
I complained, and my spirit was overwhelmed.

—PSALM 77:3 NKJV

*G*od says: You are growing up. You can no longer celebrate My love the way a little boy celebrates the care he receives from a good mother, from a tender woman who provides her child with a nutritious meal and a sweet dessert and then, after an hour of play and reading, tucks him into a warm, comfortable bed with the promise of another fun day tomorrow.

Part of growing up, of seeing Me as I am, tempts My followers to run from Me, to establish a safe distance from the distinctly unsafe and inexplicably disagreeable ways I sometimes involve Myself in the lives of those I love.

You are growing up. Your days of naive worship and shallow but exciting intimacy are over. It is always difficult for a child to become an adult, to draw close to Me as I am.

You are wrong to demand My cooperation with your understanding of life. Because I love you and because My plans for you are good, I demand your cooperation with Mine. There is no other way to enjoy My Presence.

I left Jonah with the same question I now ask you: When your life hits a bump that I could smooth but don't, will you continue to think I should surrender My wisdom to yours and do what you think best?

TAKE A MOMENT TO REFLECT

* Think of an area in your life right now that is troubling to your heart. How might you be demanding that God cooperate with your agenda?
* In that same difficult part of your life, what do you think it would look like to cooperate with God's agenda . . . today?
* What are one or two ways that you keep a safe distance from God? What fear motivates this action on your part?

TAKE A MOMENT TO PRAY

Father, Your ways are not always safe, but they are good. Expose in me those areas where I demand that You cooperate with my agenda. Teach me how to surrender to Your wisdom and Your ways. In Jesus' name, amen.

Day Eighteen: Habakkuk

YOU MUST STUMBLE BEFORE YOU DANCE

I will stand my watch
And set myself on the rampart,
And watch to see what He will say to me,
And what I will answer when I am corrected.

—HABAKKUK 2:1 NKJV

*G*od says: Never ignore your struggle with how I do things. Ask every question that rises in your heart as you live in this world. But prepare yourself to struggle even more with My response. You must stumble in confusion before you dance with joy.

Know this: those who live by faith will struggle in ways that those who live to make their lives work will never know. It is that struggle, to believe despite desperate pain and confusion that a good plan is unfolding, that will open your eyes to see Me more clearly. Is that what you want? Will you pay the price?

The price is this: you will tremble in agony as you live in a sinful, self-prioritizing world. You will learn to wait in emptiness and frustrated desire for My plan of love to reveal itself. With confidence in Me and hope in My plan, you will not only feel the pain of living in the valley but also see My glory from the mountaintop of faith.

Only those who struggle in confusion and wait in hope will be strengthened to struggle well and to wait with confidence.

Struggle well! Wait in hope!

TAKE A MOMENT TO REFLECT

❀ Identify what your normal way of thinking is in response to unexplainable circumstances and hardships. Do you plow ahead and try not to think much? Do you try to fix it? Do you try to find a Scripture passage to make sense of it? What would it look like for you to embrace before God the struggle and all that you think and feel?

❀ Based on the reading, what do you think it means to struggle well? What might have to change in your thinking?

❀ Pain in life often tempts us to believe we have done something wrong that, if corrected, would eliminate the pain. How might you think differently about suffering, given today's thoughts?

TAKE A MOMENT TO PRAY

Father God, I am not sure how to answer this question: "Am I willing to pay the price?" I want my answer to be yes, but I am scared. Strengthen my heart to believe something good is happening when pain and confusion overwhelm me. I want to learn to struggle well. In Jesus' name, amen.

Day Nineteen: Zechariah

BELIEVE WHAT YOU CANNOT SEE

Return to your fortress, O prisoners of hope; even now I
announce that I will restore twice as much to you.

—ZECHARIAH 9:12

$\mathcal{G}$od says: If you could see right now what is happening in the unseen world, you would be filled with hope.

You must trust Me for whatever tastes of glory I choose to provide in this life as you continue to build the temple. You have become a prisoner of hope. The hope I provide anchors a weary, empty, troubled soul in My plan.

Beneath difficult feelings, hope encourages by giving you reason to persevere with the joy of anticipation. Happiness depends on present blessing, which I do not guarantee. Joy depends on future hope, which I do guarantee. Do not expect to feel good. You may. You may not. My work of hope reaches into the center of your soul to strengthen your character and deepen your resolve in any circumstance of life.

I gave advance notice that My Son would come; that He would be hated and killed; that what His killers meant for evil, I meant for good; that I would then open the eyes of those I invite to the party to realize what they did in killing My Son; that I would meet them in their brokenness with a cleansing fountain; that I would then set My Son on the throne of this world, and everything would be as it should be.

Live in hope!

TAKE A MOMENT TO REFLECT

* Identify one or two ways you live to feel good. What does that look like? What prompts you to pursue feeling good in whatever way(s) you have identified?
* Think about your career, your marriage, your children, even your church. How would you define your hope in these areas? Is your hope more about happiness or true joy?
* If true hope is defined less by changed circumstances and feeling good, then it is defined more by . . . what?

TAKE A MOMENT TO PRAY

Father, I ask for eyes of faith. Help me to live by faith, anticipating a better day that is ahead while enjoying whatever blessings You choose to bestow now. May my hope be defined by the internal work You do in me rather than the external change of my circumstances. In Jesus' name, amen.

Day Twenty: Malachi

Beneath your doubt, you long for Me

---

*To you who fear My name the Sun of Righteousness
shall arise with healing in His wings.*

—Malachi 4:2 NKJV

*G*od says: I have chosen you to be part of My plan to restore this earth to its full beauty and My people to their full beauty. Your calling is to reveal My love.

You show contempt for My name when you treat Me as though I were a vending machine stocked with sweets that temporarily satisfy.

You weary Me with your idea that people enjoying the pleasant life of prosperity and peace are the real winners. Every moment spent in seizing pleasure is a moment with your back to Me.

Turn toward yourself, live for satisfaction and fullness now, and you will lose yourself.

Turn toward Me, sacrifice your pleasure for Mine, and you will find Me. You will find purpose now and joy forever.

I have loved you. I love you still. Beneath your darkness, disillusionment, and doubts, you long to know Me, to serve Me, to honor My name, to wait for Me as My prisoner of hope. That delights Me.

You are My treasure.

TAKE A MOMENT TO REFLECT

✸ In Malachi, the people repeatedly responded to God's accusation with a spirit of "What are You talking about?" Knowing this is true of us, where might you be showing contempt for God in how you live?

✸ Consider one person in your world about whom you feel jealous. What is it that drives your jealousy, and what might this jealousy be saying to God about His plan for you?

✸ God says: "Turn toward Me," instead of, "Turn toward yourself." Can you think of a way this might be practically lived out in one of your relationships today that would involve your saying no to yourself for the sake of the other?

TAKE A MOMENT TO PRAY

Father, forgive me for using You to arrange for my own pleasure and satisfaction rather than finding my pleasure and satisfaction in You. I have not recognized how I turn my back on You. I long to find my truest and most pleasurable and satisfying purpose in turning toward You in order to love another. Help me discover my deepest longing for You. In Jesus' name, amen.

Day Twenty-One:
Matthew

JESUS TAKES OVER

This is my blood of the covenant, which is poured
out for many for the forgiveness of sins.

—MATTHEW 26:28

*G*od says: I don't teach history. I *am* history. I am yesterday. I am today. I am tomorrow. Nothing I say is irrelevant. I have one plan: to bring all My people to the Great Dance, to lead them on the narrow road that moves through suffering to unimaginable joy. You must never set aside or regard as outdated anything I reveal. My later letters continue—they do not dismiss—the loving story I began to tell in My earlier ones.

I never change. I always love. I can do nothing less. I am love.

Know this: no one can pass over My first thirty-nine love letters and expect to accurately grasp and profoundly delight in the story I continue in the last twenty-seven. I want you to be caught up in the eternal story that began before time began, that develops in Genesis through Malachi, continues in Matthew through Revelation, and will continue forever when time ends.

My Son's mission was to change your life, to bring you into My kingdom of love by forgiving your self-worshipping rebellion that keeps you falling short of My way and by empowering you to bring My kingdom near to others. He never intended to keep you visibly good and pleasantly happy until heaven.

He came to reveal My nature for your sake and to change your nature for Mine.

TAKE A MOMENT TO REFLECT

❀ One of the purposes of the law and the prophets is to expose how bad things are within the hearts of God's people. Why might this be an important prelude to the introduction of Jesus in the New Testament?

❀ What do you think is involved in walking the "narrow road"? Why is it so hard to do?

❀ Our failure to live up to God's standards often results in nothing more than trying harder. This is a mistake. Look back over today's reading. What is the path that leads to entering the kingdom Jesus introduced?

TAKE A MOMENT TO PRAY

Father God, open my eyes to the whole story You are telling. Jesus said that the road is narrow. I want to be on that road. Expose where I fail to love and instead am more committed to myself. My deepest desire is to participate in Your kingdom of love. In Jesus' name, amen.

Day Twenty-Two: Mark

MOVING TOWARD THE KINGDOM

You are not far from the kingdom of God.

—MARK 12:34

*G*od says: Like you, Mark wrongly believed that the good news of following Me into kingdom living included a life blessed with a certain level of comfort and freedom from hassle. Raised in a large home where My followers were always welcomed by Mark's mother, Mary, he—like you—mixed personal comfort with spiritual reality.

But My Son moved him forward. After he repented of choosing comfort over service and suffering, Mark traveled with Peter, who couldn't stop talking about his time with My Son. Mark more fully realized that My Son lived a life of selfless servanthood that led to undeserved suffering.

He realized what kingdom living meant.

The more clearly you see Christ, the more willing you will be to suffer any loss for His sake. Kingdom living consists of radical servanthood and self-denying suffering with the hope of joy forever.

Mark finished well.

You can too.

TAKE A MOMENT TO REFLECT

❀ Around what things are your hands firmly clenched that might interfere with kingdom living? Talk to God about this and the struggle you feel to let go.

❀ What do you think is needed for you to "finish well"?

❀ Why do we believe living for God should result in personal comfort? How might your responses to personal hardship at any moment reveal what you believe about how the spiritual life should work?

TAKE A MOMENT TO PRAY

Father, what needs to change in me so that I can finish well? What do I wrongly believe about kingdom living that needs to change? I want to be moved forward. Help me to embrace suffering in a way that reveals my desire to be Your servant. In Jesus' name, amen.

Day Twenty-Three: Luke

You're standing at a crossroads

Strive to enter through the narrow gate, for many, I say to you, will seek to enter and will not be able.

—LUKE 13:24 NKJV

*G*od says: You seem to want more energy, an upbeat attitude, a fulfilling sense of personal significance. Does that describe My Son when He lived on earth?

In your heart, you rarely find a desire stronger than your wish to be satisfied with life's blessings, to feel both confident in My goodness that they'll continue and excited about life's opportunities. Your desire for spiritual formation lies on top of those self-focused desires like an attractive veneer. It needs to lie beneath them, as the controlling foundation of your life.

You are standing at a crossroads that not many reach, a crossroads where the choice between absolute surrender and lukewarm Christianity is clear. You must now determine which you want more: apparent maturity that wins recognition from others or perfect maturity that puts you in touch with desires that will remain unsatisfied until the next life.

The road to perfect maturity will make you vulnerable to severe temptations. It will stir doubts about My reality that you could avoid by choosing the easier path.

But if you want to be formed like My Son, this is the road you must choose, the one less traveled.

TAKE A MOMENT TO REFLECT

❀ Identify a time in your life when what you wanted and received left you empty. What might be the deeper desire that remained hidden beneath what you wanted and got?

❀ What makes you want to settle for a maturity that is less than what Jesus wants for you?

❀ False prophets were identified as saying, "'Peace, peace!' when there is no peace" (Jeremiah 6:14 NKJV). Well-intentioned friends sometimes seek to move us away from discouragement and despair over what we know is wrong in our hearts. At these moments, how might the "crossroad" be defined for you?

TAKE A MOMENT TO PRAY

Oh, Lord, do I really want to be formed like You? I so often choose the easier path. Give me the courage to surrender and to seek the perfect maturity that I suspect will make life more difficult. I pray in Jesus' name, amen.

Day Twenty-Four: John

THE SURPRISING ROUTE TO JOY

For as the Father raises the dead and gives life to them,
even so the Son gives life to whom He will.

—JOHN 5:21 NKJV

*G*od says: In the world you now inhabit, communion with Me is not defined by an experience of Me. Nor does it depend on blessings from Me.

To really live is to release My Son's life through yours, in any circumstance, no matter what you feel; to relate as He related, giving when no one gives back, loving when no one returns love, forgiving when no one deserves forgiveness, suffering in the place of those who should suffer.

Understand this: to commune with Me in this life is to live like My Son, with His life alive in you.

Believe this: communion with Me leads to an eternal experience of Me and unimaginable blessings from Me. You will get a taste of them now—as My Spirit chooses—and you will enjoy the banquet later when you see My Son.

Know this: heaven's reality has invaded yours. Prepare to live a new way.

Real life, the surprising route to joy, is within reach.

TAKE A MOMENT TO REFLECT

❀ How might you, in your spiritual life, be asking God for an experience of Him that really does not sustain you? (To get at this, ask yourself why you pray and what for, why you go to church, and the reason you read your Bible when you do.)

❀ How is your definition of what it means to "really live" in conflict with what is described in paragraph two?

❀ The new covenant, which Jesus came to initiate, means that the life of God, through the Spirit of the relationship of the Father and Son, now lives in you. What makes it difficult to believe that the deepest reality of your heart is that you are a lover of God?

TAKE A MOMENT TO PRAY

Father, I want to live in a new way. I want to participate in real life. You have made that possible for me through Jesus. Unearth in me the life that is deeper than my selfishness. Help me to live like Jesus, to live sacrificially and hungrily for what is yet to come. In Jesus' name, amen.

Day Twenty-Five: Acts

A NEW PURPOSE IN FREEDOM

―――――――

Daily in the temple, and in every house, they did not cease teaching and preaching Jesus as the Christ.

―ACTS 5:42 NKJV

*G*od says: What My Son began through His birth, life, death, resurrection, and ascension, He now continues.

You are not alive in this world in order to experience Me or to enjoy the blessings of a comfortable life. If that were My purpose, I'd have brought you into My Presence in heaven the moment you were forgiven and adopted into My family.

Your purpose until you die is to reveal a new attitude toward suffering and a new agenda in prayer that flows out of your new purpose in life that makes sense only if you claim your new hope of resurrection.

You are now free from slavery to the demands of self: for recognition, for life to go as you want, for good health and prosperity, for freedom from emptiness, and for the experience of fullness.

You are now free to advance the only plan whose promise of joy will be kept.

You are now free to tell people the full message of this new life.

You are now free to really live!

TAKE A MOMENT TO REFLECT

❁ What are one or two ways that you personally live to "experience" God rather than to reveal Him?

❁ Often when we hear a phrase like "really live" we are tempted to believe that this experience involves some form of a problem-free life filled with excitement and success. How would you instead define what it means to "really live" based on today's reading?

❁ Reflecting on your life, how would you put into words what your "demand of self" looks like? How does it show itself in your relationships?

❁ How would you put into words what the "new hope of resurrection" is that changes our attitude toward suffering, our agenda in prayer, and our purpose in living?

TAKE A MOMENT TO PRAY

Father, I long to *really live* in a way that is consistent with Your purposes for me. Change my perspective about suffering. Teach me to pray differently. Help me to sense the Spirit's leading in how I live. I want to work with You to advance Your kingdom. I ask this in Jesus' name, amen.

Day Twenty-Six:
Romans

DISCOVERING THE TRUTH THAT SINGS

All the nations of the world can now know the truth and be
brought into obedient belief, carrying out the orders of God,
who got all this started, down to the very last letter.

—ROMANS 16:25 MSG

*G*od says: You still tend to approach My letters the way a chess player comes to his game board. G. K. Chesterton was right when he observed that people who play chess with My truth try to get the heavens into their heads, and it's their heads that crack.

Poets, on the other hand, fill their heads with truths that lift their imaginations into the heavens. They are the grown-ups who hear the music of truth and dance like children. Do you want to discover the truth that sings?

It's time for you to pass through the corridors where truth is carefully outlined on the walls, where people take notes and mistake the truth that is living water for the dry dust of mere facts.

These parched souls endlessly analyze the composition of the water I've provided but never seem to realize it was meant for drinking.

Keep moving, not beyond truth but into truth. The corridor opens onto fields where flowers bloom and birds sing. If you listen, you can catch the scent and hear the music while you're still in the corridor.

Let the fragrance and the melody awaken your desire to drink from cool springs and stir your longing to swim in refreshing lakes. Let your time in the corridor achieve its purpose, to increase your capacity to drink more and to strengthen you to swim farther, farther away from shore, in sight of home.

TAKE A MOMENT TO REFLECT

* How would you describe the difference you hear between being a "chess player" and being a "poet"? Which one appeals to you? Why?

* Think of a time, perhaps through a passage of Scripture, where truth moved from mere fact to something that stirred a passion in you. What was it that caused this change from "dry dust" to "living water"?

* Identify for yourself what one or two truths anchor your soul, especially when hardships occur. What makes these truths alive to you? How does "living truth" affect the way you relate to others?

TAKE A MOMENT TO PRAY

Lord God, I hate that Your truth sometimes seems like dry dust. I want Your truth to penetrate into my heart and soul and affect how I live in relationship to You and others. Teach me to move into Your truth so that it becomes living water, opening my heart and mind to more than I had previously considered was possible with You. In Jesus' name, amen.

Day Twenty-Seven: 1 Corinthians

THE ONGOING MOMENT OF DECISION

Behold, I tell you a mystery: We shall not all sleep,
but we shall all be changed.

—1 CORINTHIANS 15:51 NKJV

*G*od says: The change I bring about comes slowly.

The more you attempt to hold on to your confidence in the goodness of the story I am telling, while at the same time acknowledging all that is disappointing in this life, the more you will be confronted with the ongoing moment of decision: to trust or not to trust.

Only in dark nights will hope burn bright enough to sustain your faith and release your love.

Let what you see drive you to the precipice of unbelief. Let what you feel bring you to the brink of despair.

If I exist, if I am good, if My story is loving and My plan is on course, My Spirit will speak into the deep place in your heart that only terrifying doubt renders accessible.

And in that place I will anchor you in hope.

TAKE A MOMENT TO REFLECT

* Be honest before God. What are one or two areas of significant relational disappointment in your life? What would it mean to hold on to the goodness of God as you experience the pain of each of these disappointments?

* As you consider one or two major disappointments, try to identify the lie or wrong belief that fuels your lack of trust in God. What might it look like to denounce this lie and to trust God?

* What do you think hinders you from walking perilously close to the "precipice of unbelief" and the "brink of despair" in order to hear the Spirit of hope?

TAKE A MOMENT TO PRAY

Father, help me believe that whatever negative experiences or negative emotions come my way can be opportunities to hear You and find hope. May I discover a way through them and not around them. Help me to trust that You are big enough to sustain me in my darkness. In Jesus' name, amen.

Day Twenty-Eight: 2 Corinthians

MY TRUTH REVEALS YOUR PROFOUND NEED

But in all things we commend ourselves as ministers of God . . .
sorrowful, yet always rejoicing.

—2 CORINTHIANS 6:4, 10 NKJV

*G*od says: My Spirit is telling My story to your psychological culture, a culture that actually believes woundedness—how others treat you—is a more serious problem than selfishness—how you treat others.

Understand this: no one who fails to see selfishness as his absolutely worst problem, no one who continues to believe that feelings of emptiness and pain and loneliness deserve priority attention from a grandfather-like God who simply wants all His little ones to feel good will ever know the kind of hope that energized and sustained Paul through all his disappointments and discouragement.

Paul was wonderfully encouraged when the Corinthians responded well to his earlier instructions and rebukes, but his unwavering hope remained in Me.

Live for your relational comfort, and your joy will be shallow and temporary. It will not free you to love.

Live to know the truth of My story of forgiving love, and you will be deeply unsettled by how profoundly you need forgiveness.

You will discover, slowly but surely, the power of My ongoing forgiveness and Presence to change you into a person who loves.

TAKE A MOMENT TO REFLECT

❀ Think across the spectrum of your relationships. Where are you nursing your woundedness more than seeing your selfishness? Where are you holding a grudge or keeping your distance, justifiably so in your mind?

❀ Why do you think it is easier to focus on our woundedness than to see our selfishness? What does it accomplish for us? And how does it allow us to live/relate?

❀ If our unwavering hope is not in God, what do you suspect our responses will be when people disappoint us? Conversely, if our hope is centered in God, what might our responses to the failure of others and disappointment at the hand of others look like?

TAKE A MOMENT TO PRAY

Father, forgive me for how I feel justified in my responses to the failure of others. I desire to be forgiven and to forgive others. Give me the courage to look not at others but at myself, at my defensiveness and rationalizations that feel justified. I want You to change me into a person who loves others at any cost to myself—like Jesus. In Jesus' name, I pray. Amen.

Day Twenty-Nine: Galatians

Your freedom makes you vulnerable

---

*God has called you to a free life. Just make sure that
you don't use this freedom as an excuse to do whatever
you want to do and destroy your freedom.*

—GALATIANS 5:13 MSG

*G*od says: Your preoccupation with satisfaction is the corruption beneath your compulsions. Your expectation of feeling everything you want to feel in this fallen world renders you vulnerable to false teachers who, in the name of My Son, offer you a strategy that promises to let you feel as complete now as you will feel forever in heaven.

Like My followers in the province of Galatia, you're drawn to a perversion of My story. And your freedom to love no matter how you feel is replaced by slavery to a compulsive need to feel good about yourself before you feel able to love another.

Gospel freedom means neither to indulge your whims nor to keep My rules. Whim-indulgers and rule-keepers are slaves to the corruption within that demands a kind of satisfaction My Son will not provide in this life.

My Son has set you free to love, to believe that I am good and that the good story I am telling is unfolding under His control. Faith in Me and hope for tomorrow free you to love today.

And loving with divine power releases a kind of joy into your soul that nothing else can bring.

TAKE A MOMENT TO REFLECT

❀ Identify something you do that feels compulsive or addictive. What words describe the demand (for satisfaction) that drives this particular behavior?

❀ How well do you know yourself? Are you prone more toward being a rule-keeper or a whim-indulger? How do you, in your mind, justify whichever one is true of you?

❀ How would you define the *faith* and the *hope* that free us to love? Faith in . . . ? Hope for . . . ?

TAKE A MOMENT TO PRAY

Heavenly Father, I desire to know the true freedom that Jesus came to give us. May I discover beneath my compulsions or my rule-keeping a deeper hunger for You that fuels my desire to love as Jesus loved. In His name, amen.

Day Thirty: Ephesians

Celebrate My Spirit within you

—————◆◆◆◆◆—————

Now to Him who is able to do exceedingly
abundantly above all that we ask or think, according
to the power that works in us, to Him be glory.
—Ephesians 3:20–21 NKJV

*G*od says: My enemy will stand against you at every turn. You are no match for him. But My Spirit is in you, and the enemy is no match for *Him*.

Wear the belt of truth. What My Spirit tells you will help you oppose your opposer.

Put on the breastplate of righteousness. Resolve to fight every trace of self-centeredness within you.

Identify the peace the gospel provides. Think of that peace as a pair of shoes you can wear to keep running the race in the face of all opposition.

Hold on to the shield of faith. Know that I am who I AM, that My plan is on course, that you are My child, and that one day you will be fully formed like My Son.

Keep the helmet of salvation on your head. No matter what happens, no matter how you fail, all shall be well.

Never stop reading My letters. My Word is My Spirit's sword. Use it to fight evil, first in you, then around you.

Learn to pray. Pray in My Spirit, on all occasions.

Celebrate the joy you can know when you live to complete My Son, to reveal Him to the world, and to delight Him with your response to His love.

TAKE A MOMENT TO REFLECT

❀ Jesus described the enemy as the "father of lies." What are some of the lies Satan whispers to you that threaten to overwhelm the Spirit of truth's work in you?

❀ How does knowing that God's Word is the Spirit's sword help you to understand why the order in which His work is done—"first in you, then around you"—is important?

❀ Which of the descriptions of the armor of God appeals to you today and why?

TAKE A MOMENT TO PRAY

Father, is there really a power within me that is doing more than I can think or imagine? I want to believe it and trust You. Help me to fight the battles that matter to You and let go of the ones that are not eternal. In Jesus' name, amen.

Day Thirty-One: Philippians

EMPTY, BROKEN, THIRSTY, GRATEFUL . . . AND EMPOWERED

<hr />

There's far more to this life than trusting in Christ. There's also suffering for him. And the suffering is as much a gift as the trusting.
—PHILIPPIANS 1:29 MSG

*G*od says: Never assume, as many do, that the sorrows of this life, even the severest ones, are incompatible with the joy I give.

From a heart relentlessly thirsty and filled with gratitude, Paul sang four messages of joy to the Christians at Philippi. My Spirit is singing them now to you. If you hear the music, you will be able to pour the literal life of My Son into the hearts of others.

To be content does not mean to feel content but rather to know that in My Son you have everything you need to live in rhythm with My Spirit in any circumstance of life. In emptiness and brokenness changed by My Spirit into thirst and gratitude, you are able to complete, reveal, and delight My Son.

It is empty and broken people, who at the same time are thirsty and grateful, who discover the power to live in ways they never thought possible.

TAKE A MOMENT TO REFLECT

- ❀ So often we seek ways to go *around* suffering rather than walk through it. Why do you suppose we do that, and more important, how do you attempt to skirt suffering?

- ❀ What do your mind and heart do with the sentence, "To be content does not mean to feel content"?

- ❀ Emptiness (loneliness, rejection, powerlessness) and brokenness (which means failure, specifically to love God and others) are two conditions avoided by our culture. Today's reading places a premium for believers on these two conditions. How would you equate emptiness with thirst and brokenness with gratitude?

TAKE A MOMENT TO PRAY

Lord God, I need a change of perspective. I often don't value the same things You do. Give me eyes to see the value of suffering and the importance of emptiness and brokenness. May I trust that Your life is found in the oddest places. In Jesus' name, amen.

Day Thirty-Two: Colossians

FULLY SEEN, FULLY WANTED BY AN INFLEXIBLY HOLY GOD

———❦———

He has delivered us from the power of darkness and conveyed us into the kingdom of the Son of His love, in whom we have redemption through His blood, the forgiveness of sins.

—COLOSSIANS 1:13–14 NKJV

*G*od says: Place no hope in the experience of satisfaction now. If you do, you are shifting away from the hope held out in the gospel of My Son. You will then disfigure the Christian life and blur and discount what My Son accomplished in His death and resurrection.

Right now, My Son is in you as your hope of glory, not as your opportunity to experience glory now.

That hope, when grasped, will fill you with gratitude for forgiveness. Only then will you realize that what My Son offers you now, what He is doing in you now, is far greater than the satisfying, trouble-free, always fulfilling life that you think would be best, the life that too many counselors, pastors, spiritual warfare warriors, spiritual directors, and Christian friends tell you is available now.

Consider the relationship with Me that you now possess: once alienated, now beloved; once enemies, now friends; once separated, now reconciled; once under wrath, now forgiven; once dead in selfishness, now alive in selflessness. Fully seen and fully wanted by an inflexibly holy God, who in Christ has given you the gift of absolute, secure righteousness.

That's what you have now.

Believe it. Trust it. Enjoy it.

TAKE A MOMENT TO REFLECT

❀ Ask the Spirit to reveal to you where you might be living for satisfaction now rather than in the hope held out in the gospel of Christ.

❀ Think about the times you have felt grateful to God. Is your gratitude more about a change of circumstance or a response to the forgiveness you have received? If it is more circumstantial, what does that say about how you understand what God is about in your world? In your life?

❀ Secure in your mind the last time you offered "counsel" to a friend, spouse, coworker, or child. What was the energy behind it? Was it more about a change of circumstance or leading the person to repentance for a commitment to make life work without God?

❀ Of the contrasting descriptions shared in the reading ("alienated . . . beloved," "enemies . . . friends," "under wrath . . . forgiven," etc.), which one resonates in your heart? Why?

TAKE A MOMENT TO PRAY

Father, thank You for my righteousness secured by Jesus. I long to believe not just in my head but in my heart that I am Your beloved, Your friend. Keep doing Your work so that I can more often and more consistently move from being selfish to being selfless. In Jesus' name, amen.

Day Thirty-Three:
1 Thessalonians

BLESSED BY FRUSTRATION, WEARINESS, AND FUTILITY

----

*Let us be self-controlled, putting on faith and love as a
breastplate, and the hope of salvation as a helmet. For
God did not appoint us to suffer wrath but to receive
salvation through our Lord Jesus Christ.*

—1 THESSALONIANS 5:8—9

*G*od says: Only in unplanned, unarranged, unwel-comed, unmanageable, and thoroughly unenjoyable dark nights will My plan for your maturity unfold.

Listen to what an offbeat follower of Mine, Tim Farrington, wrote in *A Hell of Mercy*: "You will be graced with the disaster your soul requires to find its way home."

John of the Cross put it this way: "No matter how much an individual does through his own efforts, he can-not actively purify himself enough to be disposed in the least degree for the divine union of the perfection of love."

Your frustration with everything, including yourself, makes it possible to turn in deeper dependence to Me. Your weariness requires the strength of supernatural love to continue serving Me. Your haunting sense of futility shuts you up to a kind of endurance that can be sustained only with hope in My Son's return.

You are in a good place.

TAKE A MOMENT TO REFLECT

❁ As you look back over the landscape of your life, where can you now see how dark nights, or what could be described as "disasters," actually became a path to maturity? How has God used these occasions to mature you? Put into words how those times changed you.

❁ Where are you frustrated with yourself, particularly in how you relate to others? What do you typically do with this frustration when it becomes apparent? How might today's reading encourage you to think differently about it?

❁ No one likes to experience frustration, weariness, or futility. Yet, if what seems like death can actually lead to life, how might these seasons of difficulty actually put you in a "good place"?

TAKE A MOMENT TO PRAY

Father, I don't like feeling frustrated or weary. And I certainly don't embrace these times. But perhaps I am missing an opportunity. Give me the eyes and the wisdom to see Your ways and how these experiences could be a "good place," a path to maturity. In Jesus' name, amen.

Day Thirty-Four:
2 Timothy

A JOY THAT FREES YOU TO ENDURE HARDSHIP

―――――――――――

The Lord will rescue me from every evil attack and will bring me
safely to his heavenly kingdom. To him be glory for ever and ever.
—2 TIMOTHY 4:18

*G*od says: The life I want you to live now is a life both to endure and to enjoy.

At times, such strong endurance will be required that joy will seem a far-off hope, a lost experience. But without endurance, you will know little of the very real joy I provide.

With endurance, a joy will develop that frees you to appreciate the pleasures of life's blessings without requiring from them a satisfaction they cannot provide.

And that same joy, more deeply felt as a longing whose complete satisfaction is guaranteed, frees you to endure whatever hardships lie ahead.

TAKE A MOMENT TO REFLECT

❀ Think of an internal struggle or perhaps a
relationship that provokes ongoing tension.
In either case, how have you given up and
settled for less than what God might want?
What would it look like to get back in the
battle and persevere?

❀ What pleasure in your life might you be
requiring to do more for you than it can? Put
words to the anger behind this demand for
satisfying pleasure.

❀ Stop and consider how you might typically
define *joy*. After reading today's thoughts, how
would you amend your understanding of joy?

TAKE A MOMENT TO PRAY

Down deep, Lord, I can sense a desire in me to persevere though I am easily derailed. Often I seek pleasure to
find an easy way out. In my heart of hearts, I long to
know the joy that Jesus knew as He endured the cross.
Make sense for me of that kind of perseverance and joy.
In His name, amen.

Day Thirty-Five:
Titus

LIVING BETWEEN TWO EPIPHANIES

---

*Denying ungodliness and worldly lusts, we should live soberly,
righteously, and godly in the present age, looking for the blessed hope
and glorious appearing of our great God and Savior Jesus Christ.*

—TITUS 2:12–13 NKJV

God says: You are living between two epiphanies. You have no higher calling in this life than to reveal the beauty of My grace until the beauty of My glory fills you with joy forever.

My high calling, the vision I am about to set before you, corresponds perfectly to your deepest desire. And My community, to the degree that it functions according to the design I make known in this letter, will release the power you need to live into My calling, to live the way you most want to live.

Sociably pleasant Christianity is no Christianity at all. It aims too low. It fails to reveal the beauty of grace.

Aim yourself and your friends toward becoming a community of men and women who long to live well consciously and intentionally, live between the two epiphanies. The way you live reveals the beauty of grace-energized relating until the beauty of glory-filled community can be enjoyed forever.

TAKE A MOMENT TO REFLECT

❀ C. S. Lewis spoke of "first and second things" as he wrote about our desires in this life. What do you suppose is the deepest (first) desire in us? What stands in the way of recognizing this desire?

❀ Identify several ways that you keep your community from being a place that releases the power needed to live out its calling.

❀ What are one or two words or phrases that describe what you think is meant by "sociably pleasant Christianity is no Christianity at all"?

TAKE A MOMENT TO PRAY

Father, as I read these words, I get a sense that my vision for what could be is too low. I want to be part of a community that is not satisfied. I want to be part of a church that understands that how we relate matters as much or more than what we know. In Jesus' name, amen.

Day Thirty-Six: Hebrews

STRENGTHENED TO BELIEVE, WAIT, AND LOVE

Because he himself suffered when he was tempted,
he is able to help those who are being tempted.

—HEBREWS 2:18

*G*od says: See Jesus, still incarnate as a human but no longer on earth, still the crucified One with nail-scarred hands and feet but no longer on the cross, still resurrected but no longer visible among you, and still ascended but no longer ascending through the devil-filled heavens.

See Jesus where He is right now.

Where He is when you awake in a cold sweat at two in the morning.

Where He is when you're alone in a hotel room and tempted to watch what should never cross the path of your eyes.

Where He is when you've been devastated by loss or rejection.

Where He is when your failure has brought you into the depths of despair.

My Son energizes you to reveal My goodness by the way you relate during difficult times.

He nourishes you, generating strength for you to believe, wait, and love.

TAKE A MOMENT TO REFLECT

❀ How do you typically handle difficult times
that come your way? Do you isolate yourself,
become short with your words, verbally bully
people, become pleasant but distant? What do
you suppose is the energy behind whatever it
is you do?

❀ During difficult times, especially those that
persist, what would have to change in you so
you could relate more like Jesus?

❀ What do you think you need in order to be
strengthened to "believe, wait, and hope"?
What does Jesus' life and/or the Scriptures say
about what you have identified that you need?

TAKE A MOMENT TO PRAY

Father, there is no one more precious to You than Your
Son. Help me to see Him as You do, in a way that would
strengthen and nourish my heart so that I could then live
and relate as He does. I ask this in His name, amen.

Day Thirty-Seven: James

SAVING YOUR SOUL FROM A WASTED LIFE

---

*Come near to God and he will come near to you . . . Humble
yourselves before the Lord, and he will lift you up.*

—JAMES 4:8, 10

God says: By faith you are already saved from an eternity without Me. You are justified before Me by faith in My Son, not by living well.

As My child, you will inherit a place in the kingdom, a seat at My table, a dance card for the party. That's My gift to you. It's guaranteed.

When you were justified before Me by faith and guaranteed heaven as My gift, My Spirit made you alive to Me with the life of My Son. He regenerated you. He gave you a new heart, a new and potentially consuming desire to love Me and others at any cost to yourself.

Justification makes you My child.

Regeneration provides the power to live like My child.

And because justification is always accompanied by regeneration, every justified person's way of relating will evidence the presence of divine life though that evidence may be visible only to Me.

When your faith leads to a consuming desire to love Me and others at any cost, when your faith is accompanied by a consistent pattern of good works, your life in this world will not be wasted, and your life in the next world will be uniquely blessed.

TAKE A MOMENT TO REFLECT

❀ Martin Luther suggested that believers are sinners and saints at the same time. If only one of these two (the saints, or lovers of God) will last for eternity, what does this say is the deepest reality of the redeemed heart? If this is true, put words to the freedom and hope that your "core reality" provides.

❀ If Jesus loved at a great cost to Himself, and if that love is the love to which we are called, how might we then define sin?

❀ Today's reading suggests that regeneration involves for each of us a "new heart, a new and potentially consuming desire to love Me and others at any cost to yourself." What then do you suppose is the believer's part in discovering this potential that is already within us?

❀ Put into your own words what it means to live a life that is not wasted.

TAKE A MOMENT TO PRAY

Father, because of Jesus it really is possible to work for Your kingdom now. Do what You must to release Your life from the depths of my soul. I want to love You and others at any cost to myself. I want to bring You pleasure and find my deepest joy in knowing You and serving You and becoming like Your Son. In His name, amen.

Day Thirty-Eight: 1 John

THE DANCE OF LOVE, THE LIFE OF JOY

---

*Whoever keeps His word, truly the love of God is perfected in
him. By this we know that we are in Him. He who says he
abides in Him ought himself also to walk just as He walked.*

—1 JOHN 2:5–6 NKJV

*G*od says: You're on the journey. You're My little child, walking the narrow road that My Son promised leads to life. You're about to learn what you've dimly known before, that when the narrow road gets especially narrow, My Spirit has a unique opportunity to do important work.

You may laugh with joy.

You may cry in hope.

You are Mine.

The life that defines My Son now defines you. You are alive in Me, to Me, and with Me.

Inexpressible joy is yours for the asking . . . on My Spirit's timetable. Never deny My Spirit's sovereignty. The divine wind of joy blows as He chooses.

And never deny your responsibility. You exist in My light. You don't always walk in My light. To walk in My light requires that you pay more attention to your failure to love than to the pain you feel when others fail to love you.

The dance of love, the life of joy that My Son and My Spirit celebrate with Me has appeared to you. My Son died to forgive you for how far short you fall of perfect love and to share the life of perfect love with you. When He returned to Me, He sent Our Spirit to pour that life into you.

And that has happened: the power to love is always in you.

TAKE A MOMENT TO REFLECT

❀ What do you think is meant by a narrowing of the narrow road? Where have you experienced this in your life? Are you aware that something deeper than your initial response to hardship might be present?

❀ The believer's responsibility is defined in today's reading by paying attention to what? Our flesh more often has us paying attention to something else. What is it? Why are we so easily distracted?

❀ Given that the power to love is already present, what is your understanding of our part in the process of experiencing its release?

❀ What makes it difficult for you to believe that you live in the power of the Son's light and that you already have the power to love? How then might true faith be defined relationally?

TAKE A MOMENT TO PRAY

I am grateful, Father, that I belong to You. So often it appears that sin is winning . . . in me and around me. Give me the faith to believe it is not, to believe that the power to love is already present in me. And give me the courage to pay more attention to my failure to love than the pain I feel that is caused by others. In Jesus' name, amen.

Day Thirty-Nine: Jude

IN BROKENNESS, YOU WILL KNOW MY POWER

Carefully build yourselves up in this most holy faith by praying in the Holy Spirit, staying right at the center of God's love, keeping your arms open and outstretched, ready for the mercy of our Master, Jesus Christ.

—JUDE 1:20–21 MSG

*G*od says: My power is sufficient to keep you from falling off the narrow road. But on that road you will feel, more acutely sometimes than at others, the unbearable ache of repeated failure to love, of always falling short of My glory.

Don't be surprised by your failure. Instead, be surprised, staggered by My response.

Only in worship will you keep yourself in My love.

Only in brokenness will you know My power to keep you from falling.

As you feel the unbearable ache of failing and being failed, I am able—if in brokenness you worship—to keep you persevering on the only road that will bring you into My Presence, full of joy and ready to dance.

Your failure provides you the opportunity to, once again, celebrate the love you taste from others but fully enjoy only from Me.

That's the gospel.

That's My story.

Contend for it with all your might.

TAKE A MOMENT TO REFLECT

❋ Do you think the ache you feel in life is more over the failures and disappointments of others, or over your failure to love others? If your deepest ache is felt when others fail you, what does this say about your understanding of sin?

❋ *Brokenness* is often misunderstood. From today's reading, how would you define its meaning? Why is that an important understanding and perhaps different from the way our culture most often uses the word?

❋ How do you think seeing our own failure frees us to enjoy the love that others offer us?

❋ How would you define the *gospel story* for which we are to contend?

TAKE A MOMENT TO PRAY

Father, I may be starting to understand why the way is narrow. It requires me to see my own failure without justification. I don't like what I see, but I am starting to believe it is the path to life. May I not fear brokenness or be surprised by my repeated failures to love. May I be surprised by Your response to how far short I fall of Your glory. In Jesus' name, amen.

Day Forty: Revelation

BECOME CAUGHT UP IN MY STORY

Whoever is thirsty, let him come; and whoever wishes,
let him take the free gift of the water of life.

—REVELATION 22:17

*G*od says: When My Son's kingdom breaks into yours, expect a collision. When His way of relating confronts the world's way of relating, all heaven and hell break loose. The battle is on, a battle to the death—and to life.

The side that appears to be losing is winning and will soon win, visibly and decisively. And the side that seems now to have the edge loses forever.

You have been seeking Me for many years. You have heard Me speak to you, and you are ready to read My final love letter to you.

Prepare to look at the reality of My kingdom as it's coming right now into your life and into this world.

Prepare to see My Son as you've never seen Him before.

Prepare to listen as the story I tell reveals the movement of history that continually brings you to a crossroad where life-altering choices are required.

I want you to do more than understand My story. I want you to be caught up in it, taking up My truth into your life. Picturing reality in graphic images penetrates through, not around, your mind and into your imagination, where true facts become living truth, experienced doctrine. Only then will My truth be taken up into your life.

There is more to reality than meets the naked eye. Only when you are gripped by what is happening in the invisible world will you live well in the visible world.

TAKE A MOMENT TO REFLECT

❀ How would you define the two kingdoms of relating that collide, ours and God's?

❀ If we as believers and as the church believed deeply that sin is not winning, how might we relate to one another differently?

❀ Why do you suppose it is easier to get caught up in the things of this life (such as a football game, music, a career, children, an addiction) than in the unfolding story that God is revealing?

❀ Reread the last sentence in today's devotional. These words imply a short-sightedness on the part of believers. Where is that the case for you? What might help you improve your vision?

TAKE A MOMENT TO PRAY

Lord Jesus, You have fought and won a battle that continues. Reveal to me where I am not in the battle, where I am fighting the wrong battles, and how I could join You in the right battle. May Your Spirit enliven my imagination with Your truth so that my heart is strengthened to believe You are winning . . . that love is winning, that Your love will fully and finally win. I pray this prayer in the powerful name of Jesus. Amen.

About the Author

*D*r. Larry Crabb is a well-known psychologist, seminar speaker, Bible teacher, author, and founder/director of NewWay Ministries. In addition to various speaking and teaching opportunities, Dr. Crabb offers a weeklong School of Spiritual Direction and a weekend conference entitled Life on the Narrow Road. He has written dozens of popular books and is a visiting professor at Richmont University in Georgia and also serves as scholar in residence at Colorado Christian University and as spiritual director for the American Association of Christian Counselors.

For additional information, please visit
www.newwayministries.org

Forever change the way you look at the Bible . . . and your own life.

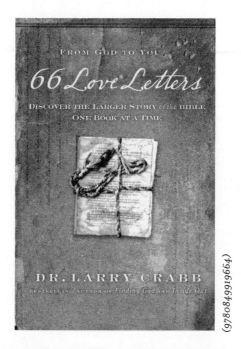

(9780849919664)

66 Love Letters *is an intimate conversation with God that invites you in. See the story of God unfold through these chapters, and you'll find not only His redeeming love but also His plan and provision designed especially for you.* 66 Love Letters *is available in jacketed hardcover, trade paper, and e-book download.*

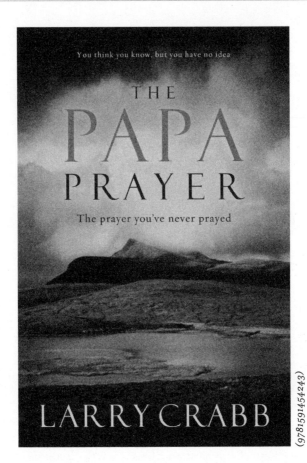

Larry invites you to begin practicing the four steps of the PAPA prayer—a revolutionary conversational approach to talking with and enjoying God. **The PAPA Prayer** *is also available in trade paper* (9780785289173) *as well as an e-book download* (9781418575779).

pass thru Gypsum

ext   133
     Dotsero
Rt. at stop sign
cross bridge (Colorado River)
sign that says
     Sweel

Rt at stop sign
  Co. River Road
     17 miles to
          Sweetwate

then go 6.8 miles
turn left at
Sweetwater Resort